140 Complete Menus

Main Dishes

3rd Edition

for Busy People

SUE GREGG

Eating Better Cookbooks

PUBLICATIONS BY SUE GREGG

The 15 Minute Meal Planner, A Realistic Approach to a Healthy Lifestyle, with Emilie Barnes, (Harvest House, 1987, 1994)

EATING BETTER COOKBOOKS
  Main Dishes, 3rd edition
  Soups & Muffins, 2nd edition
  Meals in Minutes (formerly ***Casseroles***), 3rd edition
  Lunches & Snacks, 2nd edition
  Breakfasts, 2nd edition
  Desserts, 2nd edition
  Master Index & Menu Planner
  Eating Better with Sue, Video
  Eating Better with Sue Cooking Course Workbook/Leader's Guide
  Yeast Breads, 2nd edition
  Holiday Menus
  The Creative Recipe Organizer

  Как Вам Это Нравится? *Recipes for Russian & American Appetites* with Valentina Platova

Published and distributed by
EATING BETTER COOKBOOKS
8830 Glencoe Drive
Riverside, California 92503-2135
909-687-5491
email: SueGreggsEatingBetterCookbooks@compuserve.com

Main Dishes, 3rd Edition, Copyright © 1997 by Rich & Sue Gregg
ISBN 1-878272-13-6
First Edition printed October 1987, August 1988, April 1989
Second Edition printed October 1989, August 1990, July 1991, September 1992, August 1993, June 1994
Third Edition printed October 1997

All rights reserved. No part of this book may be copied or reproduced in any form without the written consent of the publishers.

All scripture quotations, unless otherwise indicated, are taken from the HOLY BIBLE, NEW INTERNATIONAL VERSION®. NIV®. Copyright © 1973, 1978, 1984 by International Bible Society. Used by permission of Zondervan Publishing House. All rights reserved.

Disclaimer

This book is designed to provide information relating to the subject matter covered. It is sold with the understanding that the publisher and author are not engaged in rendering medical, nutritional, dietary, or other professional services. If expert assistance is required, the reader should seek the services of a competent medical professional.

This book does not cover or reprint all of the information on the subject available to the author, publisher, or the reader. Research in the field of nutrition often seems conflicting, and when hyped by media and advertising, contradictory and confusing. You are urged to read all the available material, to inform yourself as much as possible about nutrition and food preparation, and then with the advice of competent professionals to tailor the information to your personal needs.

Health is not achieved through one shot schemes, potions, or pills. It is not acquired through diet alone. Anyone who decides to pursue it must expect to invest time, effort, and discipline. We are reminded, however, that even those who inherit or achieve even the best health do not live forever. "It is appointed to man once to die..." Therefore, the reader is urged not just to prepare for the immediate, but also to discover the Creator's eternal plan through Jesus Christ.

With every edition and printing of this book every effort is made to make the information as accurate, complete, and up-to-date as possible. However, experience tells us that mistakes are inevitable in content, data caculations, and typography. This book should be used only as a general guide and not as an exacting source of information on food preparation and nutrition.

The purpose of this book is to model and motivate, to educate and entertain. The author and the publisher, shall have neither liability nor responsibility to any person or entity with respect to any loss or damage caused, alleged to be caused, directly or indirectly by the information contained in this book.

If you do not wish to be bound by the above, you may return this book to the publisher for a full refund.

What others are saying...

I go all the way now with "Eating Better." My energy level has increased greatly! Another benefit has been a 20 lb. weight loss!
Betty Lamb, Jenison, Michigan

Your recipes have really encouraged my cooking. My husband is pleased. Happy husband means a happy wife!
Christa, San Bernardino, California

You have done an excellent job presenting healthful eating with taste appeal, ease of preparation, familiar dishes, color, and beauty with thanksgiving to our God and Creator.
Kathleen Hoffman, Somerset, Wisconsin

I love your approach. You use "real people" food but it's done in a healthy way.
Lori Leeke, Plano, Texas

Your cookbooks have changed my life. Our weekly food budget has decreased from $125 to $70. I can't thank you enough.
Sheila Preston, Ontario, Canada

Your cookbooks are all I ever use. The recipes are hassle-free to make. No special ingredients to buy. They are healthy and taste great! My family loves them. Thank you for writing such wonderful books!
Chris Gordon, Everett, Washington

We've had lots of allergy problems and have been on rotation diets, vegetarian diets, combination diets, no dairy diets...Cooking became a trial to be put off as long as possible. Your books are sensible...We have only begun, but so far it is all I'd hoped for and more.
Sherry Schindler, Bartlesville, Oklahoma

I've been using the **Eating Better Cookbooks** for $1 1/2$ years. After 10 years of marriage, what a blessing to hear "This is good! This is really good!" Recipe after recipe! Praise God!
Kathie Moran, Sacramento, California

I love the cookbooks and menu planner! I've been converting recipes and using various health cookbooks for years, but these are far superior! Thanks!
Sara, Pasadena, Texas

Thank God for bringing you into our lives. When my family asks, "Whose recipe?" and I answer, "Sue Gregg's."
Johnne Neiner, Pittsfield, Massachusetts

Contents

Recipe List	1
Foreword	5
Introduction	7
Cook's Prayer	9
Nutrition Goals	10
What to Do About Salt	12
Can I Lose Weight Eating Better?	13
Using The Food Exchange System	14
Shopping	16
Ground Turkey Buying Guide	21
Investing in Cookware	22
Cancer & Heart Protective Foods	24
Vegetable Fats-Choosing Fats	26
Coping with Allergies-Modifying Recipes	28
Eating for Two (Diet Modifications during Pregnancy)	30
Menus Unlimited - 4 Week Meal Plan	32
Choices for Children - 44 Menu Choices for Children	34
Warm Weather Meals - 47 Late Spring & Summer Meals	36
Does Eating Better Really Cost More?	38
Buying Chicken	39
About Eggs	39
46 Extra Low Budget Menus	40
58 Extra Low Fat Menus	41
Planning for Extra Low Fat Dinners	42
Meals for Special Occasions - 29 Holiday & Company Meals	44
No Dairy-No Egg Meal Plan - 36 Menus	47
Lacto-Ovo-Vegetarian Menu - 52 Menus	48
What About the Vegan Vegetarian Diet? - 30 Menus	50

What About Food Combining? - 39 Menus	52
How to Read a Recipe	54
How to Read a Menu Box	55
Weights, Measures, Substitutions, Temperatures	56
About Legumes - Dried Beans & Peas	58
Bean Cookery	59
Chicken & Turkey Safety	91
Food Safety & Preservation	91
Ways to Cook Chicken or Turkey	92
About Jicama	105
About Quinoa	111
About Hot Peppers	113
About Tofu	115
About Potatoes	123
About Parsley	158
About Garlic & Onions	167
Sour Cream Alternatives	203
Broccoli Nutrients Chart	211
About Vitamin A	220
About Mushrooms	232
About Avocados	239
About Pineapple	249
Hidden Treasures of Greens, Chart	253
Whole Grain Pastas	262
Menu Extras	264
Living Bread	267
Index	269

Recipe List

QUICK RECIPES[1]

Chili*	60
Chili Con Carne*	60
Refried Beans*	64
Bean Burritos	65
Beans (Legumes), Cooked*	59
Lentil Rice Casserole*	68
Pot O' Limas*	70
Baked Potato Bar	79
Baked Potato, Gourmet	162
Roast Beef Sandwiches	81
Curried Brown Rice*	89
Baked Parmesan Chicken*	96
Javanese Dinner	101
Gazpacho	105
Mexican Rice*	107
Chicken or Tuna a la King	116
Hot Dogs, Healthier	118
Chili Dogs	118
Almond Turkey*	122
Spanish Omelette	139
Huevos Rancheros	140
Egg Foo Yung	141
Easy Lasagna*	151
Tofu Lasagna*	151
Welsh Rarebit	154
Stuffed Baked Potatoes	160
Au Gratin Baked Potatoes	162
Lemon Baked Fish*	178
Lemon Baked Salmon	179
Almond Tuna Salad	180
Turkey Burgers	185
Mexicali Burgers	186
French Fries	187
Saucy Spaghetti	194
Ragout	198
Meat Loaf*	200
Taco Chip O'le	202
Mexi Salad	204
Taco Salad	204
Almond Brown Rice*	206
Brown Rice Pilaf*	208
Baked Sweet Potatoes/Yams	220

QUICK RECIPES (Cont'd)[1]

Apple Acorn Squash	222
Honey Baked Squash	223
Fruit Bowl Meal	234
Jiffy Fruit Meal	234
Party Pizza	235
Sweet Orange Dressing	245

BEAN, MEATLESS

Baked Beans*	71
Bean Burritos	65
Beans (Legumes), Cooked*	59
Black Beans*	62
Black Beans & Rice	62
Chili*	60
Garbanzo & Pepper Curry	72
Happi's Honey Lentils*	66
Lentil Rice Casserole*	68
Lentil Rice Salad	69
Refried Beans*	64
Pot O' Limas*	70

BEEF, LAMB

Beef 'n Celery*	73
Beef Chop Suey	90
Beef Kabobs Waikiki	84
Beef Stew*	76
Beef Stir-Fry	214
Beef Stroganoff	78
Boeff Chandlier*	82
Flank Steak, Stuffed	87
Lamb, Emilie's Roast	88
Liver Louisianne	86
Roast Beef Sandwiches	81
Roast, Sue's Best*	80
Tortas (meat filling*)	74

CHICKEN, TURKEY

Almond Turkey*	122
Amandine Quiche*	134
Baked Parmesan Chicken*	96
Cashew Chicken Salad	133
Chicken a la King	116

*Freezable
[1]These are the recipes I consider quick as compared to others, but not in terms of specific number of minutes. Quick does not necessarily include baking or cooking time.

1

CHICKEN, TURKEY (Cont'd)

Chicken 'n Eggs in Bowl	99
Chicken & Pineapple Salad	131
Chicken Chop Suey	90
Chicken Curry	110
Chicken Fruit Mold	130
Chicken, Molly's	126
Chicken or Turkey Broth*	93
Chicken or Turkey Salad	132
Chicken Paprikish	98
Chicken Salad, Molly's	127
Chicken Stir-Fry	214
Chicken Tacos	104
Chicken Tostadas	103
Chili Dogs	118
Enchiladas de Pollo	112
Hawaiian Rice*	102
Hot Dogs, Healthier	118
Indonesian Summer Salad	128
Javanese Dinner	101
Lemon Herb Chicken*	94
Macaroni 'n Cheese/Franks*	153
Mizu-Taki	100
Orange Chicken	106
Pasta Salad Italian	226
Sesame Chicken*	108
Strata	120
Turkey Cutlets, Broiled	132
Turkey, Perfect Roast**	124
Yaki Tori Chicken	114
Zucchini Mexicali	97

DAIRY/CHEESE/EGG--MEATLESS

Asparagus Goldenrod	63
Baked Corn Pudding	148
Baked Potato, Au Gratin	162
Baked Potato Bar	79
Baked Potato, Broccoli-Cheese	157
Baked Potato, Gourmet	162
Baked Potato, Pizzeria	158
Baked Potato, Stuffed	160
Broccoli Cheese Casserole*	207
Broccoli Mushroom Quiche*	135
Cabbage Rolls	189
Cheese Scalloped Potatoes	166
Chiles Rellanos con Elote	147
Creamed Onions	227
Creamed Potatoes 'n Peas	175
Curried Egg Crepes	142
Egg Foo Yung	141

DAIRY/CHEESE/EGG--MEATLESS (Cont'd)

Eggplant Parmigiana	156
Fettucine*	172
Fruit Bowl Meal	234
Golden Mashed Potatoes	197
Golden Waffles	171
Guacamole Salad	229
Huevos Rancheros	140
Jiffy Fruit Bowl	234
King's Banquet Salad	224
Lasagna, Easy*	151
Lasagna, Tofu	151
Lasagna, Vegetable	150
Little Cottage Enchiladas	146
Macaroni 'n Cheese*	153
Macaroni Salad	228
Mexi Salad	204
Millet-in-a-Skillet*	218
Party Pizza*	235
Pasta Salad Italian	226
Potato Pancakes	170
Potatoes 'n Carrots Barbecue	164
Potatoes Romanoff	165
Potato Salad	168
Seven Layer Salad	225
Scalloped Potatoes	166
Spanish Omelette	139
Spinach Walnut Quiche	138
Tofu Stir Fry	215
Walnut Mushroom Casserole	152
Welsh Rarebit	154
Zesty Zucchini Bake	144
Zucchini Corn Casserole	145
Zucchini Mexicali	97

FISH

Almond Tuna Salad	180
Lemon Baked Fish	178
Lemon Baked Salmon	179
Pasta Salad Italian	226
Salmon Mousse	182
Salmon Quiche*	135
Savory Salmon Salad	181
Snappy Fillet	176
Sue's Fish Herb Seasoning	178
Tuna a la King	116
Tuna Chop Suey	90
Tuna Loaf*	174
Tuna Noodle Yummy*	173

*Freezable

GROUND TURKEY

Burger Bean Stew*	192
Chiles y Pavo con Arroz	193
Chili Con Carne*	60
Chili Con Carne, Prudence*	190
Chili Mac*	191
Good Shepherd's Pie	196
Meat Loaf*	200
Mexicali Burgers*	186
Pineapple Teriyaki Burgers	188
Ragout	198
Saucy Spaghetti	194
Saucy Spaghetti Squash	195
Seasoned Ground Turkey*	184
Sloppy Joes	200
Sweet 'n Sour Meat Balls*	201
Taco Chip O'le	202
Taco Salad	204
Turkey Burger Patties*	184
Turkey Burgers	185

VEGETARIAN NON-DAIRY

Almond Brown Rice*	206
Baked Potato Bar	79
Baked Potato es	79
Brazil Nut Stuffing/Casserole*	210
Brown Rice*	206
Brown Rice Pilaf *	208
Brown Rice Pilaf, Gourmet*	209
Brown Rice Pilaf, Savory*	209
Brown Rice, Transitional*	208
Bulgur*	111
Chop Suey w/Cashews	90
Curried Brown Rice *	89
Gazpacho	105
Golden Stuffed Potatoes	85
Hawaiian Rice/Cashew*	102
Macaroni Salad	228
Marinated Tofu Stir-Fry	115
Mexican Rice*	107
Pasta Salad Italian	226
Potato Cucumber Salad	169
Pot O' Vegetables	167
Quinoa*	111
Quinoa Curry, Toasted*	216
Ratatouille	149
Saucy Spaghetti, Meatless	194
Saucy Spaghetti Squash	195

*Freezable

VEGETARIAN NON-DAIRY (Cont'd)

Squash, Apple Acorn	222
Squash, Honey Baked	223
Squash, Cranberry Acorn	222
Stir-Fry Vegetables	213
Stuffed Green Peppers	129
Sweet Potatoes, Baked	220
Tabouli*	177
Veggi Burrito Rollups	205
Wild Rice Pilaf*	95
Yams, Baked	220
Yams in Orange Sauce	221

BREADS

Baked Brown Bread*	219
Barley Biscuits	259
Bolillos*	75
Buttered Bread Crumbs	145
Caraway Rye Bread*	256
Cornbread*	61
Crepes*	143
Good Earth Rolls*	236
French Onion Bread*	260
Hamburger Buns*	119
Hot Dog Buns*	119
Oat 'n Corn Biscuits	77
Pizza Crust*	237
Pumpernickel Bread*	258
Quiche Crusts*	136
Soup 'n Salad Croutons*	230
Buttermilk Biscuits	117

SALADS (NON-MAIN DISH)

Arranged Salads	238
Broccoli, Orange & Fig Salad	163
Carrot Salads	240
Carrot Beet Salad	240
Carrot Combo Salad	240
Carrot Zucchini Salad	240
Chop Salad	242
Cole Slaws	241
Cucumbers in Sour Cream	217
Fruit Cole Slaw	241
Garden Patch Salad	242
Garden Salad	246
Green Leaf Salad	246
Happi's Broccoli Salad	161
Holiday Cranberry Mold	251
Luau Pineapple	249

SALADS (NON-MAIN DISH, (Cont'd)

Garden Salad	246
Green Leaf Salad	246
Happi's Broccoli Salad	161
Holiday Cranberry Mold	251
Luau Pineapple	249
Marinated Cucumbers	243
Avocado-Orange Salad	232
Mixed Salads	242
Orange-Onion Salad	238
Orange-Pineapple Salad	239
Orange Tossed Salad	246
Parmesan Greens	246
Pineapple Sunshine Mold	250
Relish Tray	239
Seasonal Fruit	121
Snappy Bean Salad	230
Spinach & Orange Salad	245
Spinach-Tomato Salad	244
Spinach Salad, Chinese	244
Spinach Salad, Mid East	244
Sprout Salad	248
Three Bean Salad	243
Tomato-Avocado Salad	238
Tomato-Cucumber Salad	238
Tossed Salad	247
Tossed Salads	246
Vegetable Cole Slaw	241
Vegetable Medley	243
Waldorf Salad	242

SALAD DRESSINGS

Lemon Olive Oil Dressing	248
Marvelous Marinade	243
Oil & Vinegar Dressing	248
Poppy Seed Dressing	133
Sesame Dressing	69
Sue's House Dressing	238
Sweet Lite Dressing	141
Sweet Orange Dressing	245
Sweet Mayonnaise Dressing	141
Sweet Russian Dressing	244
Thousand Island Dressing	185

SAUCES, SPREADS, DIPS, GRAVY

Butter Spread	77
Cheese Sauce	155
Cheese Sauce, Low Fat	155
Cranberry Sauce	217

(Cont'd)

Easy Salsa	186
Enchilada Sauce*	113
Garlic Butter	261
Guacamole	229
Honey Butter Spread	261
Lemon Cream Dip	261
Mushroom Sauce	121
Roast Beef Gravy, Low Fat*	80
Saucy Spaghetti Sauce*	194
Sweet 'n Sour Sauce	212
Tartar Sauce	179
Turkey Giblet Gravy*	125
Whipped Butter	221
Yogurt-Sour Cream Blend	203

VEGETABLES

Amandine Green Beans	213
Asparagus	63
Artichokes	252
Baked Potato es	79
Broccoli	211
Broccoli Carrot Medley	183
Broccoli Cauliflower	69
Brussel Sprout s	254
Cabbage Wedges	199
Carrots Hawaiian	159
Carrots, Parsleyed	159
Corn on Cob	148
Dark Leafy Greens	253
4-Vegetable Stir Fry	83
French Fries	187
Green Beans	231
Harvard Beets	255
Julienne Cut Carrots	183
Mandarin Broccoli	67
Mashed Potatoes	123
Mushroom Saute	23
Parsnips, Dilled	87
Peppers 'n Squash Gourmet	109
Zucchini Mexicali	123

BEVERAGE

Lemon Water	266

*Freezable

Foreword

I'll never forget the time Sue Gregg shared her story in my Friday Bible Study. Two weeks earlier her three year old son had been killed in her front yard by a drunken sixteen year old driver. Sue told of how God was giving her comfort to her pain and restoration in her loss. I also sensed that her opportunity to share was part of the healing process. What neither she nor I knew was that this meeting would be the beginning of a new ministry for Sue and fresh ideas for me.

Not long after, Sue attended one of my seminars. In one short segment I described God's provision of food for our health. I demonstrated with two loaves of bread, one fluffy white and the other 100% whole wheat, by squeezing each from end to end. The fluffy white bread collapsed into a three inch mangled mass while its plastic bag swelled with air until it exploded. The 100% whole wheat bread remained unchanged.

Sue's eyes lit with attention. The point that the unlisted number one ingredient in white bread is air and what is left is calories without nutrients was not lost on her. It challenged the core of her professional assumptions. Sue's home economics training had not taught her about the difference. The demonstration revealed to her how inadequate her nutritional knowledge was.

Sue gave herself to intensive research studying the Bible to see what it had to say about food, gleaning information from books and articles on nutrition, and experimenting in her kitchen. She applied her new discoveries by transforming the quality of the ingredients in her recipes.

Both of our families benefited. First, our health reflected some dramatic improvements. Secondly, because of Sue's gift to make foods tasty, changing our eating patterns was not just a quest for health. It was an adventure in discovering God's wonderful provisions for us.

Many busy women squeezing career, family, and home into overloaded schedules opt for fast food and convenience stores. Frozen and prepackaged foods not only lack nutrients, they are too often high in sodium and cosmetic extras. The consequence is unhealthy bodies, low energy and slow minds. Help is on the Way! **Main Dishes** offers fresh ideas. They'll help you out of the meal planning rut.

I've made Sue's cookbooks part of my *Survival for Busy Women* kit. They are the tools to helping you save time as you make the transition to healthy foods. They will introduce you to quality nutrition, appetite satisfaction, and taste. Fiber and complex carbohydrate have been increased while fat and sodium have been decreased. At the same time you can be assured of adequate protein levels. Appetite satisfaction, that feeling of satiation or fullness after you've eaten, comes sooner with wholefoods than with refined products. Taste is not forgotten. You will be reminded of familiar, not strange or exotic flavors too often associated with "health foods."

You will also find that Sue has designed her recipe format to save you time. You don't have to jump back and forth between finely printed instructions and recipe ingredients. All of her recipes move sequentially down the page with ingredients bolded and instructions numbered by steps written in easily read short statements. It is an easy format to teach your children to follow. In a few short years you'll have even "more hours in your day" as they cook for you!

I'm looking forward to even more recipes from Sue's kitchen so I can test them on my family and friends. I'm eager to see the real winners in print so you can prepare them too. They'll bring you high compliments as you serve them again and again.

I've found a way to be healthier and have more time and energy to do the things that are important to me. I'm delighted to share Sue's talents with you. You will thank God as I do for her as you find more time to serve food not just as a quick filler but as a means to draw your family and friends together for opportunities to build lasting values into their lives.

You, too, will be able to say, "I've found a better way to survive as a busy woman and find *more hours in my day*!"

Emilie Barnes
MORE HOURS IN MY DAY

Introduction

The evening dinner hour brings people together. While the demands of business and school frequently threaten the sacredness of the hour, it remains the traditional time for enjoying the leisure of eating and sharing with friends and family.

I respect the value of food for what it does in drawing people together as much as for its nutritional value. The bond between mother and nursing infant is secured by food. Language is introduced to children as they are fed by parents. Family discussions teach life long values to young people around the table. Dining out for young adults develops friendship bonds and romantic relationships. Thus, emotional associations and security become closely related to food and eating experiences.

That is why we resent someone telling us that what we are eating, especially when we enjoy it, is the wrong thing to eat. This book aims to help you overcome that obstacle through a transition process. Consequently, you will find in this book a wealth of familiar American dishes using nutritionally improved ingredients. For example, you will find hot dogs and hamburgers, spaghetti and pizza, meat loaf and mashed potatoes. While new things have been added, the familiar has not disappeared.

Equally important to the value of familiar dishes is the way in which a menu is put together. There is a distinct "American" menu pattern. I have adapted that pattern to the over 140 menus presented in this book. This menu pattern blends the old and familiar with the new. It is what I call "transitional."

While food is frequently our best medicine, this book does not focus on therapeutic diets. It can be adapted, however, to meet special health needs. Food exchanges and nutrition information are given for the recipes for those who need the information. You will appreciate the suggestions given for allergies and pregnancy, and a list of cancer and heart protective foods. Nevertheless, for specific health needs requiring individualized consultation, I refer you to your physician or nutritional advisor who can help you select the best recipes and menus for your needs.

Main Dishes is a recipe book, but more than that, it is a book of complete dinner menus. Take full advantage of all the help and information that each recipe and menu offers. Read pp. 54-55, *How to Read a Recipe* and *How to Read a Menu Box,* before you begin to use them.

This book is intended to help you restore to your dining table food filled with nutritional qualities more closely representing what God put into it originally for your enjoyment and health.

In this third edition the nutrient data computer base has been completely revised to include more current data resources, and costs have been updated to 1996 average food prices. Surprisingly the food cost has not increased from the 1989 edition as we expected and our average fat percentage has dropped from 28 - 30% to 23 - 26%. Only a handful of new recipes have been added.

Enjoy with God's blessings!

Sue Gregg

Cook's Prayer

O LORD, Maker of Heaven and Earth's Land,
You made the wheat, the germ, the bran--
Nutrient and fiber-rich for the strength of man.
Cheeses 'n chicken, fish, beef, 'n dairy--
A little goes a long way to refresh the weary.

And vegetables countless--nutrient-packed treasure.
Succulent fruits for dessert: What delightful pleasure!
And nuts 'n seeds for essential fats in good measure.

Beans 'n peas for more protein and fiber, please!
With plenteous water to cook them,
Poured out by the Lord of Seas.
What great gifts, these!
Your store of food in all colors, shapes, and sizes
Are ever full of nutrient and taste surprises!

Honey dripping from the comb,
of this sweet offering could be written a tome.
Spices and herbs to jazz up flavor,
Even salt and egg yolks we count not totally
out of your favor!

Now LORD, our Maker,
Help us to put your bounty together
In balance and wholeness that we might eat better,
For bodies stronger,
And minds sharper;
For spirits assisted,
And service enlisted,
To sow the seed; to reap the harvest
From the nearest land to the farthest.

Thanks be to you, O God, Our LORD,
For food from your hand
We can afford!
Please help us to share it with our brothers and sisters,
And to serve it to our dear children.
As your Son broke 5 loaves and 2 fish
to feed more than 5,000,
So break us, LORD,
to feed more than 4 billion.

Nutritional Goals

The usual daily diet of America's millions includes 37-42% or more calories of fat, 7-14 grams dietary fiber, 450-500 mg. cholesterol, and 4000-6000 mg. sodium. Contrast those figures to the 30% or less fat (of the total calories), 10-15% protein, 55% or more complex carbohydrates, 30-40 grams dietary fiber, and 1100-3300 milligrams sodium per day--nutrient levels achieved using almost any combination of menus from the **Eating Better Cookbooks**. The data below compiled from the 140 menus in this book demonstrates our meeting these goals. See also the recipe nutrient comparison chart, **Master Index**, p. 15, and *23 Ways to Improve Your Own Main Dishes*, **Master Index**, pp. 67-68, to bring your own favorite main dishes up to meeting these nutritional standards.

GET PLENTY OF THESE (List not intended to be complete)	DAILY GOAL Amount	AVERAGE OF MAIN DISH MENUS Amount	% of Daily Goal
COMPLEX CARBOHYDRATE	55% - 65% of Calories	57% - 60% of Calories	
DIETARY FIBER	25 - 40 g[1]	15 -17 g	40-68%
VITAMIN A	RDA's[2] 5000 IU	14,000 IU	280%
VITAMIN C	60 mg[1]	94 mg	157%
VITAMIN B-1 (Thiamine)	1.5 mg	3 mg	200%
VITAMIN B-2 (Riboflavin)	1.7 mg	0.65 mg	38%
VITAMIN B-3 (Niacin)	20 mg	11 mg	55%
CALCIUM	1000 mg	340 mg	34%
POTASSIUM	3750 mg	1540 mg	41%
IRON	15 mg	9-10 mg	60-67%

[1] g = grams; mg=milligrams   [2] Recommended Daily Allowances

Nutritional Goals

Our goal is to transform the typical American high fat, low fiber diet into a higher fiber, lower fat diet. By comparing **Main Dishes** menu averages with the daily nutritional goals for dietary fiber and fat, you can observe that our main meal of the day contributes substantially. Keep in mind that these figures are realistic--not the ideal projections of a "denial" or even a therapeutic diet--based on menus eaten over a period of time. Some menus in this book fall below and some above the percentage goals. More specific information about individual items on the charts is provided elsewhere in this book.

LIMIT THESE	DAILY GOAL	AVERAGE OF MAIN DISH MENUS
PROTEIN	10% - 15% of Calories	17% of Calories
FAT (TOTAL)	30% of Calories	23% - 26% of Calories
(Saturated fat)	(10% of Calories)	(7- 8% of Calories)
(Monounsaturated fat)	(10% of Calories)	(9 -10% of Calories)
(Polyunsaturated fat)	(10% of Calories)	(8 - 9% of Calories)
CHOLESTEROL	250-300 mg	77 - 85 mg
SODIUM	2200 mg (1100-3300 mg)	843 n- 863 mg[1]
SUGAR	Reduce consumption by half (minimum goal)[2]	2 tsps.

[1] This average for sodium content reflects using all the optional salt in all the recipes. Read more about sodium, p. 12.

[2] In 1981 the average per capita sugar consumption per year was 125.6 lbs. A minimal reduction to 63 lbs. per year amounts to a little over 1/3 cup (16 tsps.) of sugar per day.

What to Do About Salt

Season all your grain offerings with salt. Do not leave the salt of the covenant of your God out of your grain offerings; add salt to all your offerings. Leviticus 2:13

There are some ingredients that can do wonders for the taste of a recipe. One of these is salt. Why? Because salt, when appropriately used, changes the very essence of the taste while not actually adding its own distinct flavor. This cannot be said for most herbs and spices which, good as they may be, merely add on their own flavor. The following are helps to control salt.

1. A number of the recipes give salt as an option. You can see the difference that using or not using the optional salt makes by comparing the total amount of sodium listed in the nutrient data at the end of the recipe. I always use the salt optionally called for. Our nutritional data for sodium (p. 11) as compared to the *Nutritional Goals* is based on using the optional salt. The average total of 843 - 863 milligrams of sodium for the dinner meal should keep you within the 1100-3300 mg. limit per day recommended by the National Academy of Sciences.

2. Using available unsalted tomato products, then seasoning to taste with salt will usually be lower in sodium than using regular tomato products which are very high in sodium (with the exception of tomato paste).

3. Tuna and canned beans, both high in sodium can be purchased with reduced salt. Canned legumes (beans and peas) can also be thoroughly rinsed to remove sodium (see *Beans*, p. 16).

4. I always use the salt called for in a new recipe on the first trial, then adjust it thereafter, to taste. Sometimes you can salt to taste while preparing the dish; but for other recipes there is no way to add salt to taste (as in bread). Note the taste of the finished product and make your salt adjustment for the next trial. Almost all of my recipes called for more salt in the original recipes than they now call for. Salt, to taste, only until the flavor of the recipe is "just right" but not actually salty.

5. When cooking or baking with butter, use unsalted butter. One tablespoon salted butter contains about 60-100 milligrams sodium depending on the brand.

6. Many common ingredients such as chicken broth, soy sauce, canned soups, mustard, catsup, and so on are being made available with less salt. Be a continual label reader for lower amounts of sodium. Adjust your recipes to taste accordingly.

7. Minimize the use of prepackaged salty snack foods, salt your recipes to a pleasing flavor, and leave the salt shaker off the table.

8. Use a high quality salt (p. 19).

See also **The 15 Minute Meal Planner**, pp. 155-158.

Calorie~Food Exchange Chart

EXCHANGES	1200 Cal	1500 Cal.	1800 Cal.	2200 Cal.
Meat	3	5	7	7
Milk	2	2	2	3
Fat	2	2	3	4
Bread	5	7	8	11
Fruit	7[1]	7[1]	9[1]	10[1]
Vegetable	5	6	6	6
Free Vegetables	Any amount of: cabbage, celery, cucumber, green onion, hot peppers, mushrooms, radishes, zucchini, salad greens, spinach			
Percentages	*19% protein 64% carb. 17% fat*	*21% protein 61% carb. 17.5% fat*	*18.5% protein 60% carb. 20% fat*	*20% protein 60% carb. 19% fat*

[1]See note, p. 14; fruit exchange allows 2 exchanges for added sweeteners on 1200, 1500 calorie limit, 3 exchanges for added sweeteners on 1800, 2200 calorie limit.

Date:_____   **PERSONAL FOOD EXCHANGE RECORD CHART**

MEAT	MILK	FAT	BREAD	FRUIT	VEG.	FREE VEG.
A						
B						

A: Enter totals eaten for the day in this row. Compare your totals with your entries in row **B**.

B: Enter level you wish to follow from *Calorie Levels Exchange Chart* above.

Shopping

You will recognize almost every ingredient used in the recipes by its generic name, such as chicken broth, worcestershire sauce, soy sauce, baking powder, flour, etc. While any form or brand of an ingredient may be used for taste, nutritional preferences are often suggested in the recipes. The following is an alphabetical list of unfamiliar ingredients and/or suggested brands. Other comparable brands may certainly be available. Ingredients are normally available in supermarkets unless "health food store" is listed. Mail order sources and food co-ops are well worth investigating locally. We have listed a few in **Desserts**, pp. 16-18, in the **Master Index**--*Updates*, including a comprehensive list of ingredients available from Trader Joe Markets (a fantastic economy resource where available), and in **The 15 Minute Meal Planner**, pp. 304-306.

Arrowroot Powder   A nutritionally superior alternative to cornstarch and used in the same way as a thickener. Purchase in spice section of supermarket, but more economical at a health food store. For more information see **Desserts**, pp. 44-45.

Beans & Peas (legumes)   Canned beans and peas are great for convenience, but more expensive than dry ones and very high in sodium. Look for 50% reduced salt brands. By thorough draining and rinsing of canned beans the sodium content may be reduced up to about 40%. Buy refried beans without lard such as *Rosarita* Vegetarian Refried Beans. Most dry beans are readily available from all sources.

Breads   Along with whole grains and flours, breads made with all whole grain flours are difficult to find in supermarkets. Health food stores are the best place to look for whole wheat hot dog and hamburger buns and high quality whole grain breads. A Trader Joe Market is a terrific resource (see above). In addition to whole grain flour, look for breads made without shortening or hydrogenated or partially hydrogenated oils. For more information see **Lunches & Snacks**, p. 147.

Butter   To reduce sodium use unsalted butter for cooking and baking. Keep frozen to prevent rancidity. See **Desserts**, p. 32, for more information.

Catsup   *Featherweight* brand at health food stores, some supermarkets.

Chicken or Beef Broth   Bouillon cubes are very high in sodium and contain MSG (monosodium glutamate). Better brands of canned broth are reduced in sodium, and omit the MSG. *Pritikin* brand is an example available in supermarkets. *Health Valley* and *Hain* brands, either salted or unsalted, are commonly available at health food stores. Trader Joe Markets (see above) also carry a much less expensive brand (fairly high in sodium however). Since salt content of these brands varies, adjust the seasoning of a recipe with salt to taste. Usually the amount of salt you add to taste will result in a lower sodium recipe than using a high sodium canned broth or bouillon cubes. The best resource economically while keeping the sodium content under control, is to make your own (see recipe, p. 93--make in quantity and freeze portions for convenience--see **Master Index**--*Subject Index*, Chicken broth.)

Chicken Franks *Health Valley* brand contains no sugar, nitrites, or pork. This brand has the best flavor of those we have tried. Health food store. See also Trader Joe Market source (see p. 16).

Cheeses (hard or "yellow") Use natural cheddars, jack, mozzarella, and Parmesan over American processed, cheese spreads, or cheese foods. There are lower sodium and lower fat cheeses available (read labels). These do not all taste equally good. Mozzarella cheese contains half the fat of other cheeses. We prefer cheese made from raw certified milk. See also **The 15 Minute Meal Planner**, pp. 125-126, 130, 132-133. Our recipe information is not based on using reduced fat or sodium hard cheeses.

Coconut Unsweetened at health food store. See **Desserts**, p. 42.

Cooking sherry wine Buy at supermarkets. Used in 3 of our over 888 recipes. Be assured, the alcohol content evaporates when cooked.

Cornmeal Cornmeal from supermarkets is "degermed" meaning that it is refined like white flour with the corn germ removed. Buy fresh stoneground cornmeal from a health food store or whole dry corn and grind it yourself in a flour mill or by the blender method (see **Meals in Minutes,** formerly **Casseroles**, p. 67, for an example.

Flour A full range of flours and/or grains to grind into flour are available at health food stores, through co-ops and mail order sources. Supermarkets generally carry only whole wheat flour, unbleached white flour, and white flour. Whole wheat pastry flour comes from soft wheat, a different variety of wheat than the hard wheat used for 100% whole wheat flour in yeast breads. Pastry flour is lower in gluten than whole wheat flour. I use pastry flour for any recipes that do not contain yeast, and whole wheat flour from hard wheat for yeast breads. Whole wheat flour can be used in any recipe, but the result will not be as light in texture as pastry flour, except for yeast breads.

I also use whole wheat pastry flour as a thickener in sauces, keeping a jar just for thickening in the refrigerator. If you use unbleached white flour in place of whole wheat flour for thickening, use just 2/3 the amount. For example, replace 3 tablespoons of whole wheat pastry flour with 2 tablespoons unbleached white flour. To substitute other kinds of flour for thickening see p. 29.

Another excellent whole wheat flour is hard white wheat (also a completely whole grain). It makes lighter yeast breads, buns, and rolls in texture and color than whole wheat flour. I especially recommend it as a more pleasing alternative for hamburger or hot dog buns and other types of dinner yeast rolls than all whole wheat, and it is a nutritionally superior alternative to using half whole wheat and half unbleached white flour. Call Walton Feed at 1-800-847-0465 to order hard white feed or to request a more local source where you may purchase it. Kamut and spelt can also be used in place of wheat flour in all baked goods (see **Breakfasts**, pp. 60-64). Keep whole grain flours on the shelf at room temperature no longer than one month. Otherwise refrigerate or freeze them, but bring to room temperature before using them in a recipe for good results.

Grains Almost any unfamiliar grain such as millet, bulgur, or quinoa can be found at a health food store. Except for brown rice, supermarkets seldom have whole grains, whole grain pastas, and whole grain breads. For the information "works" on grains see *Breakfasts*, pp. 54-85. Grains can be ordered from Jaffe Bros.--(619) 749-1133.

Herbs & Spices I use dried herbs and spices in small containers as they will lose strength of aroma and flavor over a period of time. I prefer using leaves to the ground form for some herbs, for example thyme leaves, oregano leaves, etc. All are available in supermarkets on the spice shelf. Store herbs and spices in a cool place. *Spice Garden* brand, available at health food stores, is less expensive than most supermarket brands and of excellent quality. For a mail order source see *Master Index--Updates*.

IQF (Individually Quick Frozen) Vegetables These are vegetables that are immediately processed and frozen upon harvesting and not thawed or refrozen before reaching the customer. Individual pieces are kept separated for easy removal from the bag in amount desired. Trader Joe Markets are a good resource (see p. 16).

Lecithin, Liquid Lecithin is a fat emulsifier processed from soybeans. It is very thick and viscous. It comes in dark bottles. Store at room temperature. Health food stores. Lecithin helps to dissolve cholesterol. See also *Breakfasts*, pp. 270-271.

Liquid Aminos (Bragg Liquid Aminos) An all vegetable liquid protein derived from whole soy beans and water. Delicious for broth, gravy, soups. No added salt, preservatives or chemicals. It is similar in flavor to soy sauce, but considerably milder and very low sodium. Comes in tall plastic bottles. Refrigerate after opening. Health food store. See *Breakfasts*, pp. 270-271.

Low Sodium Baking Powder Low sodium baking powder does not contain aluminum or corn. It contains less than 2 milligrams sodium per teaspoon as compared with 200 milligrams in 1 teaspoon regular baking powder. *Featherweight* is one available brand. Health food store. *Rumford*, a second choice, contains corn but not aluminum. See also *Breakfasts*, 278-280.

Mayonnaise *Hollywood* Brand at supermarkets; *Hain* brand at Health food store. Trader Joe Markets also carry their own brand (see p. 16).

Mustard *Featherweight* no salt added. Health food store or supermarket.

Nuts & Seeds Although some nuts and seeds can be purchased at supermarkets, health food stores usually have the full range of variety more economically packaged. It is also easier to find unroasted and/or unsalted nuts and seeds in the healthfood store. Roast nuts in oven at 300°F (150°C) until golden brown or over medium heat in a dry skillet when you want them roasted. Buy nuts and seeds in small quantities and keep in refrigerator or freezer. If shelled, they go rancid in a short time. Trader Joe Markets (see p. 16) is an excellent economy source for nuts.

Oils We use extra virgin olive oil, canola oil, safflower oil and flax seed oil. See pp. 26-27 for the ways in which we use these. I recommend unrefined over cold-pressed or refined oil available in supermarkets. Cold pressed oils are still highly processed as demonstrated by their pale color and weak flavor, but solvents have not been used in processing. Unrefined oils are best nutritionally. There are no preservatives in these oils, so they should be purchased in small quantities and always be refrigerated (except olive oil). Squeeze a capsule of vitamin E into an opened bottle to extend the shelf life. Health food store. For more information, recommended brands and mail order sources see p. 16, **Breakfasts**, pp. 262-268 and **The 15 Minute Meal Planner**, pp. 108-110.

Pasta or Spaghetti Sauce Compare labels and purchase the lowest in sodium content and artificial ingredients. *Healthy Choice* brand at supermarkets contains less sodium than others (390 mg. per ½ cup). *Enrico's* brand (health food store) contains 96 mg. sodium per ½ cup. *Trader Joe's* spaghetti sauces contain 510 mg. sodium per ½ cup (see p. 16).

Pastas The variety of whole grains used in pastas has mushroomed in the last few years, yet are practically non-existent in supermarkets. Through mail order sources and/or health food stores you are sure to find a variety that suits family tastes. See specifics, pp. 262-263.

Pickle Relish Honey sweetened or unsweetened. Health food store.

Rice Supermarkets carry long grain brown rice, medium grain brown rice, quick brown rice and wild rice, and *Uncle Ben's* Converted Rice (see description, p. 107). All these and more variety available in health food stores. Trader Joe Markets (see p. 16) is excellent source for best prices.

Salt All salt contains the same amount of sodium. We recommend a "sun evaporated only," or "unheated" sea salt that contains trace minerals available at health food stores. We use *RealSalt* (unrefined mineral salt), available either at health food stores or by mail from American Orsa, Inc., 75 No. State, Redmond, Utah 84652 (801) 529-7487. The cost of a high quality sea salt is inconsequential to the total food bill. We do not recommend Morton Lite Salt in place of salt. See also p. 12, pp. and **The 15 Minute Meal Planner**, 155-158.

Sour Cream Light sour cream contains half the fat of sour cream. *Knudsen's NiceN' Light* brand contains cultured grade A pasteurized milk, nonfat milk, cream, kosher gelatin, vegetable enzyme. Fat free sour cream, now available is another option; however, we prefer the taste results of half light sour cream and half plain nonfat yogurt to fat free sour cream. Experiment with tastes.

Spike Seasoning Our favorite all purpose seasoning, *Spike*, contains 39 herbs and spices and is about half sodium. It should not be used for the purpose of cutting down on sodium. Health food store and supermarkets.

Soy Sauce A good soy sauce should be naturally brewed, that is, fermented. *Kikkoman* Lite Soy Sauce contains 200 milligrams sodium per teaspoon. *Kikkoman* Milder Soy Sauce contains slightly less, but the difference is not worth the additional cost. Regular soy sauce contains 314 milligrams sodium per teaspoon. Kikkoman contains wheat. If you are allergic to wheat, *Tamari* brand (health food stores) contains no wheat (with 313 milligrams sodium per teaspoon).

Sue's Kitchen Magic Seasoning A wonderful seasoning made from wheat, soy, corn, and alfalfa, this seasoning imparts a salty flavor. It is a hydrolyzed vegetable protein, but contains only natural MSG which is not usually a problem. One teaspoon contains 840 milligrams of sodium. When used in recipes, the addition of salt (2,132 mg. sodium per teaspoon) can usually be reduced. See also *Master Index--Updates*. To purchase, see order form in back of this book.

Sweeteners In *Main Dishes* we use honey or crystalline fructose (available at health food stores). For more information see *Breakfasts*, p. 15.

Taco Chips Purchase taco, tortilla, or corn chips made from stoneground or whole corn, polyunsaturated and unhydrogenated oil such as safflower or canola oil. Baked without oil, salted, unsalted and reduced salt (such as 20%, 25%, or 40% less salt) are also available. Our preference is to mix half regular salted chips and half baked chips purchased from Trader Joe Markets (see p. 16). Avoid partially hydrogenated oil, shortening, and coconut oil. Health food store and some supermarkets.

Tomato Products No salt and salt reduced brands are becoming more available in supermarkets. Adjust salt seasoning in recipes to taste depending on the brand you use.

Tofu Most supermarkets have tofu, regular or soft. Main dish recipes call for regular tofu. Tofu with an unrefrigerated shelf life of 10 months is available. One such brand is *Mori Nu*, in 10.5 oz. packages. Tofu made from ogranically grown soy beans is available in some health food stores.

Tortillas   Purchase corn tortillas made with stoneground or whole corn, lime, and water and whole wheat tortillas (or chapatis). Health food store, some supermarkets. Beware of "whole wheat" tortillas in supermarkets. that contain part white flour (still a better option than white flour torillas) and partially hydrogenated vegetable shortening (the bad news).

Tuna Fish Buy water packed. It not only reduces fat and calories, It also retains from 12-22% more omega-3 fatty acids (good for the heart) since the oil in oil packed tuna (usually soybean oil) draws more omega-3's out of the tuna than water does, and is drained off. Sodium or salt reduced tuna is available in many supermarkets (see p. 180 for some examples). *Featherweight* is a no salt brand available at some health food stores.

Wheat Germ Wheat germ goes rancid in a very short time. Buy vacuum packed *Kretchemer* brand (supermarket in cereals section). Refrigerate or store in freezer after opening. See *Breakfasts*, p. 273, for more information.

Worcestershire Sauce *Robbie's* or *Life All Natural* brands at health food stores.

Yogurt   Look for any of the following terms on the label: active cultures, viable cultures, live bacteria, thermophilus acidophilus, lactobacillicus acidophilus, bifidus. These terms identify the presence of live bacteria that assist the colon in producing its own live bacteria. Supermarkets and health food stores (Also Trader Joe Markets--see p. 16). For more information see *Breakfasts*, pp. 26-27.

Ground Turkey Buying Guide

The chart below compares various available fat levels of cooked ground turkey and ground beef. Turkey skin added to ground turkey accounts for the variety of fat levels. Package label advertising emphasizes fat percentage of raw meat by weight, not calories, although the law now requires the fat percentage of daily food value to be listed on the standardized nutrition information label. For a full explanation of this standardization see ***The 15 Minute Meal Planner***, pp. 292-302. Both are confusing. The percentage of fat in calories of a given cooked portion is the most useful. Select ground turkey lowest in calories of fat that is available to you and that is acceptable to your family tastes. For the purpose of most widely acceptable flavor balanced with economy the *Turkey Store* brand, "7% fat" (by weight) has been selected as the basis for the nutrition information in our recipes using ground turkey, . The use of 99% fat free ground turkey will further reduce fat levels of all ground turkey recipes (and will increase cost). Favorable options have increased over the years, including favorable ground beef options.

3 oz. cooked (85 grams)	Calories	Protein grams	Fat grams	Fat % of Calories	Fat % of Weight	Cost 1996[8]
Grd Turkey, extra lean breast[1]	113	25.4	1.4	11%	1.6%[7]	$3.59
Grd Turkey, lean[2]	160	25	5.7	32%	6.7%	$2.49
Grd Turkey, "7%" fat[3]	174	25	8.7	45%	10%[7]	$1.99
Grd Turkey, *Louis Rich*	186	19.6	11.8	57%	13.9%	$1.39
Grd Beef, "7%" Fat[4]	175	23.7	8.3	42%	9.7%[7]	$2.79
Grd Beef, "15%" Fat[4]	256	23.5	18.1	56.5%	21%[7]	$1.96
Grd Beef, reg.	243[5] 260[6]	22.9[5] 20.3[6]	16.1[5] 19.2[6]	59.6%[5] 66.5%[6]	18.9%[5] 22.6%[6]	$1.59

[1]*Turkey Store* brand, "99% fat free"   [2]*Jennie-O Natural Choice* brand

[3]*Turkey Store* brand, "7% fat"   [4]*Moran's* brand

[5]***Jean Carper's Total Nutrition Guide***, 1989, p. 336--fried well done; [6]fried medium

[7]Fat % of cooked weight is higher than fat % of raw meat because moisture is lost in cooking which concentrates same amount of fat in less weight when no fat is drained off. Package labels give fat percentages based on raw, not cooked meat.   [8]Cost per lb. raw

Cancer & Heart Protective Foods

God saw all that he had made, and it was very good. Genesis 1:31

Research reveals that certain food groups in sufficient dietary amounts can reduce risk of heart disease and cancer. These foods contain one or more protective nutrients (i.e. antioxidants as vitamins C and E, and beta carotene) and properties (i.e. phytochemicals in plants that give them color, aroma and flavor; see **Master Index**, p. 61). These foods provide a composite of nutritive and non-nutritive elements that undoubtedly work together synergistically (for definition, see **Breakfasts**, p. 55). This is why it is so important to eat the whole foods, such as those listed below.

Cancer Protective Foods

Vegetables high in **beta carotene:**
(provitamin A):
    dark greens, carrots,
    red peppers,
    apricots, peaches,
    yellow squash,
    sweet potatoes or
      yams (USA variety)

Vegetables containing
indoles, isothiocyanates:
    cruciferous: cabbage,
    brussel sprouts,
    broccoli, kohlrabi,
    cauliflower

Vegetables high in **chlorophyll:**
    parsley; dark leafy greens: 
      spinach, kale,
      chard,
      collard greens,
      mustard greens,
      turnip greens

High **flavonoids, vitamin C** foods:
    lemons, limes, oranges,
    grapefruit, tomatoes,
    pumpkins, potatoes,
    strawberries,
     green and red peppers

Foods with **protease inhibitors:**
    pumpkin seeds, sunflower
    seeds, soybeans

Allium vegetables: 
    garlic, onions,
    leeks,
    chives,
    scallions

High **calcium** foods: 
    lowfat or nonfat
    yogurt, nonfat
    milk, lowfat or nonfat
    cottage cheese,
    buttermilk

High **vitamin E** foods containing **selenium:**
    whole grains,
    wheat germ,
    nuts, seeds,
    fresh vegetables

Oils high in **monounsaturated fat:**
    olive oil, canola oil
Oils high in **essential fatty acids:**
    flax seed oil, sunflower oil,
    corn oil, safflower oil,
    soybean oil